3/13

W9-CCM-503

BEYOND
Heaven's
DOOR

MAX LUCADO

THOMAS NELSON
Since 1798

NASHVILLE   DALLAS   MEXICO CITY   RIO DE JANEIRO

© 2013 Max Lucado

Selections in this book are taken from the previously published *When Christ Comes* by Max Lucado,
© 1999 Max Lucado.

Published in Nashville, Tennessee, by Thomas Nelson. Thomas Nelson is a registered trademark
of Thomas Nelson, Inc.

Thomas Nelson, Inc. titles may be purchased in bulk for educational, business, fund-raising,
or sales promotional use. For information, please e-mail SpecialMarkets@ThomasNelson.com.

Unless otherwise noted, Scripture quotations are taken from the New Century Version®, © 2005
by Thomas Nelson. Used by permission. Other Scripture references are from
the following sources: *The Message* by Eugene H. Peterson (MSG), © 1993, 1994, 1995, 1996, 2000,
2001, 2002. Used by permission of NavPress Publishing Group. All rights reserved. Holy Bible, New
International Version®, NIV® (NIV). © 1973, 1978, 1984 by Biblica Inc.™ Used by permission of
Zondervan. All rights reserved worldwide. New King James Version® (NKJV), © 1982 by Thomas
Nelson, Inc. Used by permission. All rights reserved. Holy Bible, New Living Translation (NLT),
© 1996. Used by permission of Tyndale House Publishers, Inc., Wheaton, Illinois 60189. All rights
reserved. *The Jerusalem Bible* (TJB). © 1966 by Darton, Longman & Todd Ltd. and Doubleday &
Company, Inc. Used by permission. *The Living Bible* (TLB), © 1971. Used by permission of Tyndale
House Publishers, Inc., Wheaton, Illinois 60189. All rights reserved. *Good News Bible: The Bible
in Today's English Version* (TEV), © 1976, 1992 by the American Bible Society. Used by permission.
J. B. Phillips: The New Testament in Modern English, Revised Edition (PHILLIPS), © J. B. Phillips 1958,
1960, 1972. Used by permission of Macmillan Publishing Co., Inc. Revised Standard Version of
the Bible (RSV), © 1946, 1952, 1971, 1973 by the Division of Christian Education of the National
Council of the Churches of Christ in the USA. Used by permission.

Literary development and design: Koechel Peterson & Associates, Inc., Minneapolis, Minnesota.

Library of Congress Control Number: 2012952800

ISBN 9780849948436

Printed in the United States of America

13 14 15 16 17 18 QG 6 5 4 3 2 1

And I heard a loud voice
from the throne, saying,
"Now God's presence is with people,
and he will live with them,
and they will be his people.
GOD HIMSELF WILL BE WITH THEM
AND WILL BE THEIR GOD."

REVELATION 21:3

CONTENTS

ADMISSION
at the Door

Not all those who say
"You are our Lord"
will enter the kingdom of heaven.

MATTHEW 7:21

I MAKE no claims to being a good golfer, but I readily confess to being a golf addict. If you know of a twelve-step program for the condition, sign me up. "Hi, I'm Max. I'm a golfaholic." I love to play golf, watch golf, and on good nights, I even dream golf.

Knowing this will help you appreciate the extreme joy I felt when I was invited to attend the Masters Golf Tournament. A pass to the Masters is the golfer's Holy Grail. Tickets are as scarce as birdies on my scorecard. So I was thrilled. The invitation came via pro golfer Scott Simpson. Each player is given a certain number of passes, and Scott offered Denalyn and me two of his. (If there was ever any question about Scott's place in heaven, that gesture erased the doubt.)

So off we went to Augusta National Golf Club in Augusta, Georgia, where golf heritage hangs like moss from the trees. There you find the green where Nicklaus sank the putt. The fringe where Mize holed the chip. The fairway where Saranson hit the approach shot. I was a kid in a candy store. And like a kid, I couldn't get enough. It wasn't enough to see the course and walk the grounds; I wanted to see the locker room. That's where the clubs of Hogan and Azinger are displayed. That's where the players hang out. And that's where I wanted to be.

But they wouldn't let me.

To be turned away from seeing golf history is one thing, but to be refused admission into heaven is quite another.

A guard stopped me at the entrance. I showed him my pass, but he shook his head. I told him I knew Scott, but that didn't matter. I promised to send his eldest child through college, but he didn't budge. "Only caddies and players," he explained. Well, he knew I wasn't a player or a caddie. Caddies at the Masters are required to wear white coveralls. My clothing was a dead giveaway. So I left, figuring I'd never see the clubhouse. I had made it all the way to the door but was denied entrance.

Many people fear the same will happen to them in heaven. They fear being turned away at the door. A legitimate fear, don't you think? We're talking about a pivotal moment. To be turned away from seeing golf history is one thing, but to be refused admission into heaven is quite another.

That is why some people don't want to discuss heaven. It makes them nervous. They may be God-fearing and church-attending people but still nervous. Is there a solution for this fear? Need you spend the rest of your life wondering if you will be turned away at the door?

According to the Bible, it is possible to "know beyond the shadow of a doubt that you have eternal life" (1 John 5:13 MSG). How? How can any of us know for sure?

Curiously, it all has to do with the clothing we wear.

A STRICT
Dress Code

*Friend, how were you
allowed to come in here?
You are not dressed
for a wedding.*

MATTHEW 22:12

JESUS TOLD the parable of a king who planned a wedding party for his son. Invitations were given, but the people "refused to come" (Matt. 22:3). The king is patient and offers another invitation. This time the servants of the king are mistreated and killed. The king is furious. The murderers are punished, the city is destroyed, and the invitation is re-extended, this time to everyone.

The application of the parable is not complicated. God invited Israel, his chosen ones, to be his children. But they refused. Not only did they refuse, they killed his servants and crucified his Son. The consequence was the judgment of God. Jerusalem was burned, and the people were scattered.

As the parable continues, the king offers yet another invitation. This time the wedding is opened to everyone—"good and bad" (Matt. 22:10), or Jews and Gentiles. Here is where we non-Jews appear in the parable. We are the beneficiaries of a wide invitation. And someday we will stand at the entryway to the king's castle. But the story doesn't end there. Standing at the doorway is not enough. A certain wardrobe is required. The parable ends with a chilling paragraph.

Let's pick up
the story at the end
of verse 10:

AND THE WEDDING HALL WAS FILLED WITH GUESTS. WHEN THE KING CAME IN TO SEE THE GUESTS, HE SAW A MAN WHO WAS NOT DRESSED FOR A WEDDING. THE KING SAID, "FRIEND, HOW WERE YOU ALLOWED TO COME IN HERE? YOU ARE NOT DRESSED FOR A WEDDING." BUT THE MAN SAID NOTHING. SO THE KING TOLD SOME SERVANTS, "TIE THIS MAN'S HANDS AND FEET. THROW HIM OUT INTO THE DARKNESS, WHERE PEOPLE WILL CRY AND GRIND THEIR TEETH WITH PAIN." (MATT. 22:10–13)

Jesus loved surprise endings, and this one surprises . . . and frightens. Here is a man who was at the right place, surrounded by the right people, but because he wore the wrong clothing, he was cast from the presence of the king.

"Wrong clothes? Max, are you telling me that Jesus cares what clothes we wear?"

Apparently so. In fact, the Bible tells us exactly the wardrobe God desires.

"But clothe yourselves with the Lord Jesus Christ and forget about satisfying your sinful self" (Rom. 13:14).

"You were all baptized into Christ, and so you were all clothed with Christ. This means that you are all children of God through faith in Christ Jesus" (Gal. 3:26–27).

Standing at the doorway is not enough. A certain wardrobe is required.

This clothing has nothing to do with dresses and jeans and suits. God's concern is with our spiritual garments. He offers a heavenly robe that only heaven can see and only heaven can give. Listen to the words of Isaiah: "The Lord makes me very happy; all that I am rejoices in my God. He has covered me with clothes of salvation and wrapped me with a coat of goodness" (Isa. 61:10).

Remember the words of the father when the prodigal son returned? He wanted his son to have new sandals, a new ring, and what else? New clothes. "Bring the best clothes and put them on him" (Luke 15:22). The father wanted the son to have the best clothing available.

Your Father wants you to have the same.

FIX YOUR
Wardrobe

*Live in him so that
when Christ comes back,
we can be without fear
and not be ashamed
in his presence.*

1 JOHN 2:28

MOST OF us could use some help with our wardrobes, but this discussion of clothing has nothing to do with what the store sells you. It has everything to do with what God gives you when you give your life to him. Let me explain.

When a person becomes a follower of Christ, when sins are confessed and the grace of Jesus is accepted, a wonderful miracle of the soul occurs. The person is placed "in" Christ. The apostle Paul described himself as "a man in Christ" (2 Cor. 12:2). When he described his colleagues, he called them "fellow workers in Christ Jesus" (Rom. 16:3 NIV). The greatest promise is extended not to the wealthy or educated but to those who are "in Christ." "Therefore, there is now no condemnation for those who are *in Christ Jesus*" (Rom. 8:1 NIV, emphasis mine). John urges us to "live in him so that when Christ comes back, we can be without fear and not be ashamed in his presence" (1 John 2:28).

What does it mean to be "in Christ"? The clothing illustration is a good one. Why do we wear clothes? There are parts of our body we want to hide.

The same can be true with our spiritual lives. Do we want God to see everything about us? No. If he did, we would be fearful and ashamed. How could we ever hope to go to heaven with all our mistakes showing? "The true life," Paul wrote, "is a hidden one in Christ" (Col. 3:3 PHILLIPS).

Let's take this a step further.

Let's imagine how a person who isn't wearing the clothing of Christ appears in the eyes of heaven. For the sake of discussion, envision a decent human being . . . we'll call him Danny Decent. Danny pays his taxes, pays his bills, pays attention to his family, and pays respect to his superiors. He is a good person. In fact, were we to dress him, we would dress him in white.

But heaven sees Danny differently. God sees what you and I miss. For every time Mr. Decent sins, a stain appears on his clothing. For example, he stretched the truth when he spoke to his boss yesterday. He was stained. He fudged, ever so slightly, on his expense report. Another stain. The other guys were gossiping about the new employee, and he chimed in. Still another. What God sees is a man clothed in mistakes.

Unless something happens, Danny will be the man in the parable, the one without the wedding garment. The wedding garment, you see, is the righteousness of Christ. And if Danny faces Christ wearing his own decency instead of Christ's goodness, he will hear what the man in the parable heard: "'You are not dressed for a wedding.' . . . So the king told some servants, 'Tie this man's hands and feet. Throw him out into the darkness, where people will cry and grind their teeth with pain'" (Matt. 22:12–13).

The true life is a hidden one in Christ.

What happens if Danny changes his clothes? What if he agrees with Isaiah, who said, "Our righteous acts are like filthy rags" (Isa. 64:6 NIV)? Suppose he goes to Christ and prays, "Lord, take away these rags. Clothe me in your grace." Suppose he confesses the prayer of this hymn: "Naked, come to thee for dress, helpless, look to the for grace."[1]

If he does, here is what happens. Jesus, in an act visible only to the eyes of heaven, removes the robe of stains and replaces it with his robe of righteousness. As a result, Danny is clothed in Christ. And, as a result, Danny is dressed for the wedding.

To quote another hymn: "Dressed in His righteousness alone, faultless to stand before the throne."[2]

Do we want God to see
everything about us?

No. If he did,
we would be fearful
and ashamed.

COLOR
Matters

*They will walk with me
and will wear white clothes,
because they are worthy.*

REVELATION 3:4

GOD HAS only one requirement for entrance into heaven: that we be clothed in Christ.

Listen to how Jesus described the inhabitants of heaven: "Those who win the victory will be dressed in white clothes like them. And I will not erase their names from the book of life, but I will say they belong to me before my Father and before his angels" (Rev. 3:5).

Listen to the description of the elders: "Around the throne there were twenty-four other thrones with twenty-four elders sitting on them. They were dressed in white and had golden crowns on their heads" (Rev. 4:4).

And what is the clothing of the angels? "The armies of heaven, dressed in fine linen, white and clean, were following him on white horses" (Rev. 19:14).

All are dressed in white. The saints. The elders. The armies. How would you suppose Jesus is dressed? In white?

You'd think so. Of all the people worthy to wear a spotless robe, Christ is. But according to the Bible he doesn't.

THEN I SAW HEAVEN OPENED, AND THERE BE-
FORE ME WAS A WHITE HORSE. THE RIDER ON THE
HORSE IS CALLED FAITHFUL AND TRUE, AND
HE IS RIGHT WHEN HE JUDGES AND MAKES
WAR. HIS EYES ARE LIKE BURNING FIRE, AND
ON HIS HEAD ARE MANY CROWNS. HE HAS A
NAME WRITTEN ON HIM, WHICH NO ONE BUT
HIMSELF KNOWS. HE IS DRESSED IN A ROBE
DIPPED IN BLOOD, AND HIS NAME IS THE
WORD OF GOD. (REV. 19:11–13)

Why is Christ's robe not white? Why is his garment dipped in blood? Let me answer by reminding you what Jesus did for you and me. Paul said simply, "He changed places with us" (Gal. 3:13).

He did more than remove our coat; he put on our coat. And he wore our coat of sin to the cross. As he died, his blood flowed over our sins. They were cleansed by his blood. And because of this, when Christ brings us to heaven, we have no fear of being turned away at the door.

Speaking of being turned away at the door, I'm sure you are dying to hear whether I made it into the locker room at the Masters Golf Tournament. Well, I did.

The day prior to the tournament, the golfers play an exhibition round on a par-three course. It is customary for the golfers to give their caddies the afternoon off and invite friends or family members to take their places. Well, Scott invited me to be his caddie. "Of course, you'll have to wear the white overalls," he explained.

And, of course, I didn't mind. *Snicker.*

That afternoon, I made my way to the clubhouse. And through the same door, walking past the same guard, I stepped into the golfers' inner sanctum. What made the difference?

Simple. I was wearing the right clothes.

Jesus did more than remove our coat of sin; he put on our coat and wore it to the cross.

THE BRAND-NEW
You

There is an order to this resurrection:
Christ was raised as the first of the harvest;
then all who belong to Christ
will be raised when he comes back.

1 CORINTHIANS 15:23 **NLT**

SUPPOSE YOU are walking past my farm one day and see me in the field crying. Concerned, you approach me and ask what is wrong. I look up and extend a palm full of seeds in your direction. "My heart breaks for the seeds."

"What?"

Between sobs I explain, "The seeds will be placed in the ground and covered with dirt. They will decay, and we will never see them again."

As I weep, you are stunned. You look around for a turnip truck, off which you are confident I tumbled. Finally, you explain to me a basic principle of farming: out of the decay of the seed comes the birth of a plant.

You kindly remind me: "Don't you know that you will soon witness a mighty miracle of God? Given time and tender care, this tiny kernel will break from its prison of soil and blossom into a plant far beyond its dreams."

Any farmer who grieves over the burial of a seed needs a reminder: a time of planting is not a time of grief. Any person who anguishes over the burial of a body may need the same. We may need the reminder Paul gave the Corinthians: "There is an order to this resurrection: Christ was raised first of the harvest; then all who belong to Christ will be raised when he comes back" (1 Cor. 15:23 NLT).

Between the death of the body

of a Christian and the return of our Savior, Scripture assures us that the soul is living, but the body is buried. This is an intermediate period in which we are "away from this body and . . . at home with the Lord" (2 Cor. 5:8).

Upon our physical death, our souls will journey immediately to the presence of God while we await the resurrection of our bodies. And when will this resurrection occur? You guessed it. When Christ comes. "When Christ comes again, those who belong to him will be raised to life, and then the end will come" (1 Cor. 15:23–24).

What does Paul mean, "those who belong to him will be raised to life"? What will be raised? My body? If so, why *this* body? I don't like my body. Why don't we start over on a new model?

Come with me back to the farm, and let's look for some answers.

If you were impressed with my seed allegory, I stole the idea from the apostle Paul. The fifteenth chapter of his first letter to the Corinthians is the definitive essay on our resurrection. He wrote:

BUT SOMEONE MAY ASK,

"HOW ARE THE DEAD RAISED? WHAT KIND OF BODY WILL THEY HAVE?" FOOLISH PERSON! WHEN YOU SOW A SEED, IT MUST DIE IN THE GROUND BEFORE IT CAN LIVE AND GROW. AND WHEN YOU SOW IT, IT DOES NOT HAVE THE SAME "BODY" IT WILL HAVE LATER. WHAT YOU SOW IS ONLY A BARE SEED, MAYBE WHEAT OR SOMETHING ELSE. BUT GOD GIVES IT A BODY THAT HE HAS PLANNED FOR IT.

I CORINTHIANS 15:35–38

In other words, you can't have a new body without the death of the old body.[1] Or as Paul said, "When you sow a seed, it must die in the ground before it can live and grow" (v. 36).

A friend told me that Paul's parallel between seeds sown and bodies buried reminded her of a remark made by her youngest son. He was a first grader, and his class was studying plants about the same time the family attended a funeral of a loved one. One day, as they were driving past a cemetery, he pointed and said, "Hey, Mom, that's where they plant people."

The apostle Paul would have liked that. In fact, he would like us to change the way we think about the burial process. The graveside service is not a burial but a planting. The grave is not a hole in the ground but a fertile furrow. The cemetery is not the resting place but the transformation place.

Upon death, our souls
will journey immediately
to the presence of God
while we await
the resurrection
of our bodies.

THE ULTIMATE
Triumph

*No one has ever
imagined what God
has prepared for those
who love him.*

1 CORINTHIANS 2:9

MANY PEOPLE assume that death has no purpose. It is to them what the black hole is to space—a mysterious, inexplicable, distasteful, all-consuming power. Avoid it at all costs. And so we do all we can to live and not die. God, however, says we must die in order to live. When you sow a seed, it must die in the ground before it can grow (1 Cor. 15:36). What we see as the ultimate tragedy, he sees as the ultimate triumph.

And when a Christian dies, it's not a time to despair but a time to trust. Just as the seed is buried and the material wrapping decomposes, so the fleshly body will be buried and will decompose. But just as the buried seed sprouts new life, so the body will blossom into a new body. As Jesus said, "Unless a grain of wheat falls into the earth and dies, it remains a single grain of wheat; but if it dies, it brings a good harvest" (John 12:24 PHILLIPS).

If you'll permit a sudden shift of metaphors, let me jump from plants to dinner and dessert. Don't we love to hear the cook say, "As soon as you are finished, I have a surprise for you"? God says something similar regarding the body. "Let's finish with the one you have, and then I have a surprise."

What is this surprise?

When a Christian dies, it's not a time to despair but a time to trust.

What is this new body I will receive? Again, our seed analogy helps. Paul wrote, "When you sow it [the seed], it does not have the same 'body' it will have later" (1 Cor. 15:37). Meaning, we can't envision the new body by looking at the old body.

I think you'll appreciate the way Eugene Peterson paraphrases this text:

THERE ARE NO DIAGRAMS FOR THIS KIND OF THING. WE DO HAVE A PARALLEL EXPERIENCE IN GARDENING. YOU PLANT A "DEAD" SEED; SOON THERE IS A FLOURISHING PLANT. THERE IS NO VISUAL LIKENESS BETWEEN SEED AND PLANT. YOU COULD NEVER GUESS WHAT A TOMATO WOULD LOOK LIKE BY LOOKING AT A TOMATO SEED. WHAT WE PLANT IN THE SOIL AND WHAT GROWS OUT OF IT DON'T LOOK ANYTHING ALIKE. THE DEAD BODY THAT WE BURY IN THE GROUND AND THE RESURRECTION BODY THAT COMES FROM IT WILL BE DRAMATICALLY DIFFERENT. (1 COR. 15:36–37 MSG)

Paul's point is clear. You can't envision the glory of the plant by staring at the seed, nor can you garner a glimpse of your future body by studying the present one. All we know is that this body will be changed.

GROANING
in the Tent

He will transfigure
these wretched bodies
of ours into copies
of his glorious body.

PHILIPPIANS 3:21 TJB

IF YOU'RE like me, you're asking this question now: "Come on, Paul, can you give us just a hint? Tell us a little more about our new bodies."

Apparently he knew we would ask, for the apostle stayed on the subject for a few more paragraphs in 1 Corinthians 15 and provides one final point: you may not be able to envision it, but one thing's for sure; you are going to love your new body.

Paul outlines three ways God will transform your body. Your body will be changed from

1. Corruption to incorruption—"The body is sown in corruption, it is raised in incorruption" (v. 42 NKJV).

2. Dishonor to glory—"It is sown in dishonor, it is raised in glory" (v. 43 NKJV).

3. Weakness to power—"It is sown in weakness, it is raised in power" (v. 43 NKJV).

Corruption. Dishonor. Weakness. Three unflattering words are used to describe our bodies. But who would argue with them?

Julius Schniewind didn't. He was a highly regarded European Bible scholar. In the final weeks of his life, he battled a painful kidney disease. His biographer tells how he was putting on his coat to go home. As he did, the severe pain in his side caused him to groan aloud the Greek phrase "*Soma tapeinōseōs.*" The student of Scripture was quoting the words of Paul: "For our citizenship is in heaven, from which we also eagerly wait for the Savior, the Lord Jesus Christ, who will transform our lowly body [*soma tapeinōseōs*]" (Phil. 3:20–21 NKJV).[1]

You and I don't go about mumbling Greek phrases, but we do know what it is like to live in a lowly body. In fact, some of you know all too well. Your body is so tired, so worn. Joints ache and muscles fatigue. You understand why Paul described the body as a tent. "We groan in this tent," he wrote (2 Cor. 5:2). Your tent used to be sturdy and strong, but the seasons have passed, the storms have raged, and your tent is not as strong as it used to be.

Or, then again, maybe your tent, your body, never has been strong. Your sight never has been crisp; your hearing never has been clear. Your walk never has been sturdy; your heart never has been steady. You've watched others take for granted the health you've never had. You'd give anything, yes, anything, for one full day in a strong, healthy body.

Corruption. Dishonor. Weakness.

Three unflattering words
used to describe our bodies.

BUT WHO WOULD ARGUE WITH THEM?

If that describes you, let God speak to your heart for just a moment. The purpose of this book is to use the reality of heaven to encourage the heart. Few people need encouragement more than the physically disabled. And few verses encourage more than Philippians 3:20–21. We read through the first part of verse 21 a few paragraphs ago; you'll relish the complete verse: "He will take these dying bodies of ours and change them into glorious bodies like his own" (Phil. 3:21 TLB).

The promise is your body will be changed.

You will not receive a different body; you will receive a renewed body. Just as God can make an oak out of a kernel or a tulip out of a bulb, he makes a *new* body out of the old one. A body without corruption. A body without weakness. A body without dishonor. A body identical to the body of Jesus!

My friend JONI EARECKSON TADA was rendered a quadriplegic by a teenage diving accident, and her last four decades have been spent in discomfort. She, more than most, knows the meaning of living in a lowly body. At the same time, she, more than most, knows the hope of a resurrected body in heaven.

Listen to her words:

"Somewhere in my broken,
   paralyzed body is the seed
of what I shall become."

"The paralysis makes what I am to become all the more grand when you contrast atrophied, useless legs against splendorous resurrected legs. I'm convinced that if there are mirrors in heaven (and why not?), the image I'll see will be unmistakably 'Joni,' although a much better, brighter Joni. So much so, that it's not worth comparing. . . . I will bear the likeness of Jesus, the man from heaven."[2]

I will bear the likeness...

LIKE
Jesus

*People who belong to the earth
are like the first man of earth.
But those people who belong to heaven
are like the man of heaven.
Just as we were made like the man of earth,
so we will also be made
like the man of heaven.*

1 CORINTHIANS 15:48–49

WOULD YOU like a sneak preview of your new body? We have one by looking at the resurrected body of our Lord. After his resurrection, Jesus spent forty days in the presence of people. The resurrected Christ was not in a disembodied, purely spiritual state. On the contrary, he had a body—a touchable, visible body.

Just ask Thomas. Thomas said he wouldn't believe in the resurrection unless "I . . . put my finger where the nails were and put my hand into his side" (John 20:25). The response of Christ? He appeared to Thomas and said, "Put your finger here, and look at my hands. Put your hand here in my side. Stop being an unbeliever and believe" (v. 27).

Jesus didn't come as a mist or a wind or a ghostly specter. He came in a body. A body that maintained a substantial connection with the body he originally had. A body that had flesh and bones. For did he not tell his followers, "A spirit has not flesh and bones as you see that I have" (Luke 24:39 RSV)?

Jesus' resurrected body, then, was a real body, real enough to walk on the road to Emmaus, real enough to appear in the form of a gardener, real enough to eat breakfast with the disciples at Galilee. Jesus had a real body.[1]

At the same time, this body was not a clone of his earthly body. Mark tells us that Jesus "appeared in another form" (Mark 16:12 RSV). While he was the same, he was different. So different that Mary Magdalene, his disciples on the sea, and his disciples on the path to Emmaus did not recognize him. Though he invited Thomas to touch his body, he passed through a closed door to be in Thomas's presence.[2]

So what do we know about the resurrected body of Jesus? It was unlike any the world had ever seen.

What do we know about our resurrected bodies? They will be unlike any we have ever imagined.

Will we look so different that we aren't instantly recognized? Perhaps. (We may need name tags.) Will we be walking through walls? Chances are we'll be doing much more.

God is going to renew your body and make it like his. What difference should this make in the way you live?

Our resurrected bodies will be unlike any we have ever imagined.

You will live forever in this body. It will be different, mind you. What is now crooked will be straightened. What is now faulty will be fixed. Your body will be different, but you won't have a different body. You will have this one. Does that change the view you have of it? I hope so.

God has a high regard

for your body. You should as well. Respect it. I did not say worship it. But I did say respect it. It is, after all, the temple of God (1 Cor. 6:19). Be careful how you feed it, use it, and maintain it. You wouldn't want anyone trashing your home; God doesn't want anyone trashing his. After all, it is his, isn't it? A little jogging and dieting to the glory of God wouldn't hurt most of us. Your body, in some form, will last forever. Respect it.

Remember: you will be like Jesus.

YOUR PAIN WILL *not* LAST FOREVER.

BELIEVE IT.

Your arthritic joints won't be in heaven.

Your weak heart will be strong in heaven.

There is no cancer in heaven.

Your new body will have a new mind. No disjointed thoughts. No memory failure.

You will be like Jesus.

A DAY
of Rewards

When the master comes
and finds the servant
doing his work,
the servant will be blessed.

MATTHEW 24:46

IT'S SUNDAY, September 27, 1998. Even though the St. Louis Cardinals have no hope of making the Major League Baseball playoffs, the ballpark is packed. It was packed three weeks earlier when Mark McGwire tied Roger Maris's home run record with a 430-foot shot off the stadium club window. For thirty-seven years, no one had hit more than sixty-one homers in one season; now the St. Louis slugger has hit sixty-eight. And he isn't finished. Number sixty-nine lands in the left field seats. It takes two curtain calls to silence the crowd. Home run number seventy comes in the seventh inning. The fans are on their feet before he comes to bat; they stay on their feet long after he crosses the plate.

They cheer the home run. They cheer the new record. And they cheer something else.

I'm speculating now. But I really believe that they—and we—cheered something else. We cheered because he did what we wanted to do. Wasn't there a younger, more idealistic you who dreamed of hitting the big ball? Or winning the Pulitzer? Or singing on Broadway? Or receiving the Nobel Peace Prize? Or clutching an Oscar?

But most of us don't make it.

Bats are traded for calculators or stethoscopes or computers. And, with only slight regret, we set about the task of making a living. We understand. For every million who aspire, only one achieves. The vast majority of us don't hit the big ball, don't feel the ticker tape, don't wear the gold medal, don't give the valedictory address.

And that's okay. We understand that in the economy of earth, there are a limited number of crowns.

The economy of heaven, however, is refreshingly different. Heavenly rewards are not limited to a chosen few but "to all those who have waited with love for him to come again" (2 Tim. 4:8). The three-letter word *all* is a gem. The winner's circle isn't reserved for a handful of the elite but for a heaven full of God's children who "will receive the crown of life that God has promised to those who love him" (James 1:12 NIV).

Those who went unknown on earth will be known in heaven.

From the mouth of Jesus, we hear a similar promise: the saved of Christ will receive their reward. "When the master comes and finds the servant doing his work, the servant will be blessed" (Matt. 24:46).

The promise is echoed in an epistle: "The Lord will reward everyone for whatever good he does, whether he is slave or free" (Eph. 6:8 NIV).

And in a beatitude: "Rejoice and be glad, because great is your reward in heaven" (Matt. 5:12 NIV).

For all we don't know about the next life, this much is certain. The day Christ comes will be a day of reward. Those who went unknown on earth will be known in heaven. Those who never heard the cheers of men will hear the cheers of angels. The small will be great. The forgotten will be remembered. The unnoticed will be crowned, and the faithful will be honored. What McGwire heard in the shadow of the St. Louis Arch will be nothing compared to what you will hear in the presence of God. McGwire received a Corvette. You'll receive a crown—not just one crown, but three. Would you enjoy a preview?

THE CROWN
of Life

*Blessed is the man
who perseveres under trial,
because when he has stood the test,
he will receive the crown of life
that God has promised
to those who love him.*

JAMES 1:12 NIV

TO HELP you appreciate eternity, consider this rule of thumb: *heaven will be wonderful not only because of what is present but also because of what is absent.*

As the apostle John took notes on what he saw in heaven, he was careful to mention what was absent. Remember his famous list of "no mores"? God "will wipe away every tear from their eyes, and there will be no more death, sadness, crying, or pain, because all the old ways are gone" (Rev. 21:4).

Did you catch the first "no more"? *There will be no more death.* Can you imagine a world with no death, only life? If you can, you can imagine heaven. For citizens of heaven wear the crown of life.

What have you done today to avoid death? Likely a lot. You've popped pills, pumped pecs, passed on the pie, and pursued the polyunsaturates. (Please pardon the perpetuity of *P*s in that sentence.) Why the effort? Because you are worried about staying alive. That won't be a worry in heaven.

God "will wipe away every tear from their eyes, and there will be no more death, sadness, crying, or pain, because all the old ways are gone" (REV. 21:4).

In fact, you won't be worrying at all. Some of you moms worry about your kids getting hurt. You won't worry in heaven. In heaven we'll feel no pain. Some of you fellows worry about getting old. You won't in heaven. We'll all be ceaselessly strong. You travelers worry about the plane crashing. You won't in heaven. Heaven has no planes that I know of. If it does, they don't crash. But if they crash, no one dies. So you don't have to worry.

Years ago I hurt my back. The injury was nothing serious but enough to wake me up. I needed to get in better shape. So I set out on an exercise regimen that was, if I say so myself, pretty strict. In time the back muscles were strengthened, my weight was down, and I was feeling pretty strong—when I came very close to losing it all. A lady ran a red light and nearly hit me. As I was driving away, this goofy thought popped in my head: *Is that my reward for all my exercise? I mean, I run, eat right, lift weights, and, through no fault of my own, it could be gone in a second.*

Isn't that the way life goes?

We are frail creatures. Consider the mother who gives birth, only to be rewarded with a stillborn child. Consider the man who works hard to retire, only to have retirement cut short by cancer. Consider the high school athlete who trains hard, only to be injured. We are not made of steel; we are made of dust. And this life is not crowned with life; it is crowned with death.

The next life, however, is different. Jesus urged the Christians in Smyrna to "be faithful, even if you have to die, and I will give you the crown of life" (Rev. 2:10).

THE CROWN
of Righteousness

Now, a crown is being held for me—
a crown for being right with God.
The Lord, the judge who judges rightly,
will give the crown to me on that day.

2 TIMOTHY 4:8

BESIDES THE crown of life, the apostle Paul suggests a second crown we'll receive in heaven:

> I have done my best in the race, I have run the full distance, and I have kept the faith. And now there is waiting for me the victory prize of being put right with God, which the Lord, the righteous Judge, will give me on that Day—and not only to me, but to all those who wait with love for him to appear. (2 Tim. 4:7–8 TEV)

The word *righteousness* defines itself. It means, simply, to be in a right relationship with God. The apostle Paul looks toward the day when he is crowned in righteousness. Now, the careful Bible student might raise a question here. *Aren't we already righteous? Didn't I just read previously that we are clothed in righteousness when we become Christians?* Yes, you did.

Then why do we also receive crowns of righteousness? What happens in heaven that hasn't happened on earth? Those are good questions and can be answered by using a favorite analogy of the apostle Paul: the analogy of adoption.

While we lived in Rio de Janeiro, we met several American families who came to Brazil to adopt children. They would spend days, sometimes weeks, immersed in a different language and a strange culture. They fought the red tape and paid the large fees, all with the hope of taking a child to the United States.

Can you imagine a world minus sin?

In some cases the adoption was completed before the child was born. For financial reasons, the couple would often have to return to the US while awaiting the birth of their child. Think about their position: The papers have been signed, the money has been given, but the child is not yet born. They must wait until the birth before they can return to Brazil and claim the child.

Hasn't God done the same for us? He entered our culture, battled the resistance, and paid the unspeakable price that adoption required. Legally we are his. He owns us. We have every legal privilege accorded to a child. We are just waiting for him to return. We are, as Paul said, "waiting for God to finish making us his own children" (Rom. 8:23).

We are in a right relationship now; we are clothed with Christ. But when Jesus comes, the relationship will be made even "righter." (I know that's not a word.) Our wardrobe will be complete. We will be crowned with righteousness. We will be rightly related to God.

Think about what that means. What prevents people from being rightly related to God? Sin. And if heaven promises a right relationship with God, what is missing in heaven? You got it, baby. Sin. Heaven will be sin free. Both death and sin will be things of the past.

Is this a big deal?

I think so. Earlier we tried to imagine a world with no death; let's do the same with sin. Can you imagine a world minus sin? Have you done anything recently because of sin?

At the very least, you've complained. You've worried. You've grumbled. You've hoarded when you should have shared. You've turned away when you should have helped. You've second-guessed, and you've covered up. But you won't do that in heaven.

Because of sin, you've snapped at the ones you love and argued with the ones you cherish. You have felt ashamed, guilty, bitter. But you won't have those feelings in heaven.

Because of sin, the young

are abused and the elderly forgotten. Because of sin, God is cursed and drugs are worshiped. Because of sin, the poor have less and the affluent want more. Because of sin, babies have no daddies and husbands have no wives. But in heaven, sin will have no power; in fact, sin will have no presence. There will be no sin.

Sin has sired a thousand heartaches and broken a million promises. Your addiction can be traced back to sin. Your mistrust can be traced back to sin. Bigotry, robbery, adultery—all because of sin. But in heaven, all of this will end.

Can you imagine a world without sin? If so, you can imagine heaven.

BECAUSE OF SIN

Let me make this promise more practical. Some time ago a friend asked a very honest question about eternity. It had to do with his ex-wife. She is now a Christian, and he is now a Christian. But things are still icy between them. He wondered how he would feel when he saw her in heaven.

I told him he would feel great and be thrilled to see her. Why? Well, what causes tension between people? In a word, *sin.* If there is no sin, there is no tension. None. No tension between ex and ex, between black and white, between abused and abuser, even between the murdered and the repentant murderer.

The beautiful prophecy of Isaiah 11 will come true: "Then wolves will live in peace with lambs, and leopards will lie down to rest with goats. Calves, lions, and young bulls will eat together, and a little child will lead them" (Isa. 11:6).

Almost a millennium later, John made a similar promise. Heaven will be great, he said, not just because of what is present but because of what is missing. God "will wipe away every tear from their eyes, and there will be no more death, sadness, crying, or pain, because all the old ways are gone" (Rev. 21:4).

John's list could have gone on forever. Since heaven has no sin or death there will be no more _____. You fill in the blank. No more aspirin. Chemotherapy. Wheelchairs. Divorce. Jail cells or broken hearts. Crippled limbs or car wrecks.

To be crowned in life means no more death. To be crowned in righteousness means no more sin. And to be crowned in glory means no more defeat.

MAX LUCADO

SIN HAS SIRED

A THOUSAND HEARTACHES

AND BROKEN

A MILLION PROMISES.

THE CROWN
of Glory

When the Chief Shepherd appears,
you will receive the crown of glory
that will never fade away.

1 PETER 5:4 NIV

I HAVE a special word to a special group. Some of you have never won a prize in your life. Oh, maybe you were quartermaster in your Boy Scout troop or in charge of sodas at the homeroom Christmas party, but that's about it. You've never won much. You've watched the stars of this world carry home the trophies and walk away with the ribbons. All you have are "almosts" and "what ifs."

If that hits home, then you'll cherish this promise: "And when the Chief Shepherd appears, you will receive the crown of glory that will never fade away" (1 Peter 5:4 NIV).

Your day is coming. What the world has overlooked, your Father has remembered, and sooner than you can imagine, you will be blessed by him. Look at this promise from the pen of Paul: "God will praise each one of them" (1 Cor. 4:5).

What an incredible sentence! *God will praise each one of them.* Not "the best of them" or "a few of them" or "the achievers among them," but "God will praise each one of them."

You won't be left out. God will see to that. In fact, God himself will give the praise. When it comes to giving recognition, God does not delegate the job. God himself does the honors. God himself will praise his children.

And what's more, the praise is personal!

Paul wrote, "God will praise each one of them" (1 Cor. 4:5). Awards aren't given a nation at a time, a church at a time, or a generation at a time. The crowns are given one at a time. God himself will look you in the eye and bless you with the words, "Well done, good and faithful servant! You have been faithful with a few things; I will put you in charge of many things. Come and share your master's happiness!" (Matt. 25:23 NIV).

With that in mind, let me urge you to stay strong. Don't give up. Don't look back. Let Jesus speak to your heart as he says, "Hold on to what you have, so that no one will take your crown" (Rev. 3:11 NIV).

WHEN IT COMES TO GIVING RECOGNITION,

God does not delegate the job.

GOD HIMSELF WILL PRAISE HIS CHILDREN.

A DAY OF
Sweet Surprises

*You are our hope, our joy,
and the crown
we will take pride in
when our Lord Jesus Christ comes.*

1 THESSALONIANS 2:19

OSKAR SCHINDLER had his share of less-than-noteworthy characteristics. He was a womanizer and a heavy drinker. He bribed officials and was a member of the German Nazi Party. But buried in the dark of his heart was a diamond of compassion for the condemned Jews of Krakow, Poland.

The ones Hitler sought to kill, Schindler sought to save. He couldn't save them all, but he could save a few, and so he did what he could. What began as a factory for profit became a haven for eleven hundred fortunate souls whose names found their way onto his list—Schindler's list.

If you saw the movie by the same name, you'll remember how the story ends. With the defeat of the Nazis came the reversal of roles. Now Schindler will be hunted, and the prisoners will be free. Oskar Schindler prepares to slip into the night. As he walks to his car, his factory workers line both sides of the road. They have come to thank the man who saved them. One of the Jews presents Schindler with a letter signed by each person, documenting his deed. He is also given a ring, formed out of the gold extracted from a worker's tooth. On it is carved a verse from the Talmud, "He who saves a single life saves the world entire."

In that moment, in the brisk air of the Polish night, Schindler is surrounded by the liberated. Row after row of faces. Husbands with wives. Parents with children. They know what Schindler did for them. They will never forget.

What thoughts raced through Schindler's mind in that moment? What emotions surface when a person finds himself face-to-face with lives he's changed?

Someday you'll find out. Schindler saw the faces of the delivered; you will too. Schindler heard the gratitude of the redeemed; you'll hear the same. He stood in a community of rescued souls; the same is reserved for you.

When will this occur? It will occur when Christ takes you to heaven. The promise of 1 Thessalonians 2:19 isn't limited to the apostle Paul. I'll explain. "You are our hope, our joy, and the crown we will take pride in when our Lord Jesus Christ comes" (1 Thess. 2:19).

It was about six months

since Paul had left Thessalonica. He, Timothy, and Silas had spent three fruitful weeks in the city. The result of their stay was a nucleus of believers. Luke provided a one-sentence profile of the church when he wrote: "Some of them [the Jews] were convinced and joined Paul and Silas, along with many of the Greeks who worshiped God and many of the important women" (Acts 17:4).

An eclectic group attended the first church service: some were Jews, some were Greeks, some were influential females, but all were convinced that Jesus was the Messiah. And in a short time, all paid a price for their belief. Literally. The young believers were dragged into the presence of the city leaders and forced to post bond for their own release. That night they had helped Paul, Timothy, and Silas sneak out of the city.

Paul moved on, but part of his heart was still in Thessalonica. The little church was so young, so fragile, but oh-so-special. Just the thought of those believers made him proud. He longed to see them again. "We always thank God for all of you and mention you when we pray" (1 Thess. 1:2). He dreamed of the day he might see them again and, even more, dreamed of the day they would see Christ together.

Note what he said to them: "You are our hope, our joy, and the crown we will take pride in when our Lord Jesus Christ comes" (1 Thess. 2:19). The verse conjures up an image akin to the one of Schindler and the survivors. An encounter between those freed and the one who led them to freedom. A moment in which those saved can meet the one who led them to salvation.

In this case Paul will meet with the Thessalonians. He will search the sea of faces for his friends. They will find him, and he will find them. And in the presence of Christ, they will enjoy an eternal reunion.

The same will be true for you on that day!

What emotions surface when a person finds himself face-to-face with lives he's changed?

OH HAPPY
Day

The master answered,
"You did well.
You are a good and loyal servant.
Because you were loyal with small things,
I will let you care for much greater things.
Come and share my joy with me."

MATTHEW 25:23

THINK ABOUT the day Christ comes. There you are in the great circle of the redeemed in heaven. Your body has been made new—no more pain or problems. Your mind has been made new—what you once understood in part, you now understand clearly. You feel no fear, no danger, no sorrow. Though you are one of a throng, it's as if you and Jesus are all alone.

And he asks you this question. I'm speculating now, but I wonder if Christ might say these words to you: "I'm so proud that you let me use you. Because of you, others are here today. Would you like to meet them?"

Chances are you'd be surprised at such a statement. It's one thing for the apostle Paul to hear such words. He was an apostle. We can imagine a foreign missionary or famous evangelist hearing these words—but us?

Most of us wonder what influence we have. Most of us can relate to the words of Matthew 25: "Master, what are you talking about?" (v. 44 MSG).

At that point Jesus might—again, these are wild speculations—but Jesus might turn to the crowd and invite them. With his hand on your shoulder, he announces, "Do we have any here who were influenced by this child of mine?" One by one, they begin to step out and walk forward.

God implants such passion.

The first is your neighbor, a crusty old sort who lived next door. To be frank, you didn't expect to see him. "You never knew I was watching," he explains, "but I was. And because of you, I am here."

And then comes a cluster of people, a half dozen or so. One speaks for the others and says, "You helped out with the youth devotional when we were kids. You didn't open your mouth much, but you opened your house. We became Christians in your living room."

The line continues. A coworker noticed how you controlled your temper. A receptionist remarks on how you greeted her each morning. Someone you don't even remember reminds you of the time you saw her in the hospital. You came to visit a friend in the next bed, but on the way out you stopped and spoke a word of hope with this stranger who looked lonely.

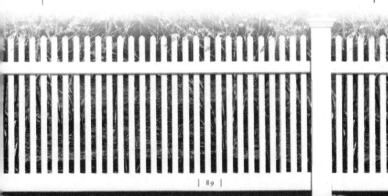

You are most amazed by the people from other countries. After all, you never even traveled to Asia or Africa or Latin America, but look! Cambodians, Nigerians, Colombians. How did you influence them? Christ reminds you of the missionaries who came your way. Your friends said you had a soft spot for them. You always gave money. "I can't go, but I can send," you'd say. Now you understand; you didn't have a soft spot. You had the Holy Spirit.

It's not long before you and your Savior are encircled by the delightful collection of souls you've touched. Some you know, most you don't, but for each you feel the same. You feel what Paul felt for the Thessalonians: pride. You understand what he meant when he said: "You are our hope, our joy, and the crown we will take pride in when our Lord Jesus Christ comes" (1 Thess. 2:19). Not a haughty, look-what-I've-done pride. But rather an awestruck joy that declares, "I'm so proud of your faith."

But Jesus isn't finished.

He loves to save the best for last, and I can't help but imagine him doing the same in heaven. There is one more group. And Jesus parts the crowd so you will see them.

Your family.

Your spouse is the first to embrace you. There were times when you wondered if either of you would make it. But now you hear the words whispered in your ear: "Thanks for not giving up on me."

Then your parents. No longer frail, as you last saw them, but robust and renewed. "We're proud of you," they say. Next come your children. Children for whom you cared and over whom you prayed. They thank you; over and over they thank you. They know how hard it was and how hard you tried, and they thank you.

And then some faces you don't recognize. You have to be told—these are grandchildren and great-grandchildren and descendants you never saw until today. They, like the others, thank you for an inherited legacy of faith.

They thank you.

Will such a moment occur? I don't know, but it's possible!

"I'M SO PROUD THAT YOU LET ME USE YOU.
BECAUSE OF YOU,
OTHERS ARE HERE TODAY.
WOULD YOU LIKE TO MEET THEM?"

NO
Regrets

For to me, to live is Christ,
and to die is gain.

PHILIPPIANS 1:21 NKJV

ON THE day you are reunited in heaven with your loved ones and those you influenced with your faith, you can be certain of two things. First, its grandeur and glory will far outstrip any description these words can carry: "No one has ever imagined what God has prepared for those who love him" (1 Cor. 2:9). And that "no one" certainly includes this one.

Second, if such a moment of reunion occurs as I described it, you can be certain you won't regret any sacrifice you made for the kingdom. The hours of service for Christ? You won't regret them. The money you gave? You'd give it a thousand times over. The times you helped the poor and loved the lost? You'd do it again.

Oskar Schindler, whom I told you about previously, would have. Earlier we wondered about Schindler's final thoughts. We wondered how he felt, surrounded by the Jewish people he had saved from the Holocaust. His last appearance in the movie gives us a good idea. There, in the presence of the survivors, he tucks the letter they gave him away in his coat. He accepts the ring and looks from face to face. For the first time, he shows emotion. He leans toward Isaac Stern, the factory foreman, and says something in a voice so low, Stern asks him to repeat it. He does. "I could have done more," he says, gesturing toward a car he could have sold. "That would have released ten prisoners." The gold pin on his lapel would have bribed an official to release two more. In that moment, Schindler's life is reduced to one value. Profit is forgotten. The factory doesn't matter. All the tears and tragedy of the nightmare are distilled into one truth. People. Only one thing counts—people.

I suggest you'll feel the same in heaven.

Oh, you won't feel the regrets. Heaven knows no regret. Our God is too kind to let us face the opportunities we missed. But he is happy to let us see the ones we seized. In that moment, when you see the people God let you love, I dare say, you'd do it all again in a heartbeat.

You'd change the diapers, fix the cars, prepare the lessons, repair the roofs. One look into the faces of the ones you love, and you'd do it all again.

In a heartbeat . . . a heavenly heartbeat.

*People.
Only one
thing counts—
people.*

SEEING
Jesus

*We know that
when Christ comes again,
we will be like him,
because we will see him as he really is.*

1 JOHN 3:2

AUGUSTINE ONCE posed the following experiment. Imagine God saying to you, "I'll make a deal with you if you wish. I'll give you anything and everything you ask: pleasure, power, honor, wealth, freedom, even peace of mind and a good conscience. Nothing will be a sin, nothing will be forbidden, and nothing will be impossible to you. You will never be bored, and you will never die. Only . . . you will never see my face."[1]

The first part of the proposition is appealing. Isn't there a part of us, a pleasure-loving part of us, that perks up at the thought of guiltless, endless delight? But then, just as we are about to raise our hands and volunteer, we hear the final phrase, "You will never see my face."

And we pause. *Never?* Never know the image of God? Never, ever behold the presence of Christ? At this point, tell me, doesn't the bargain begin to lose some of its appeal? And doesn't the test teach us something about our hearts? Doesn't the exercise reveal a deeper, better part of us that wants to see God?

For many it does.

For others, however, Augustine's exercise does not raise interest as much as it raises a question. An awkward question, one you may be hesitant to ask for fear of sounding naive or irreverent. Since you may feel that way, why don't I ask it for you? At the risk of putting words in your mouth, let me put words in your mouth. "What's the big deal?" you ask. "No disrespect intended. Of course I want to see Jesus. But to see him *forever*? Will he be that amazing?"

According to Paul, he will. "On the day when the Lord Jesus comes," he wrote, "all the people who have believed will be amazed at Jesus" (2 Thess. 1:10).

Amazed at Jesus.

Not amazed at angels or mansions or new bodies or new creations. Paul didn't measure the joy of encountering the apostles or embracing our loved ones. If we will be amazed at these, which certainly we will, he did not say. What he did say is that we will be amazed at Jesus.

What we have seen only in our thoughts, we will see with our eyes. What we've struggled to imagine, we will be free to behold. What we've seen in a glimpse, we will then see in full view. And, according to Paul, we will be amazed.

What we've seen in a glimpse,
we will then see in full view.
And we will be amazed.

THE AMAZING
One

When I saw him,
I fell down at his feet
like a dead man.
He put his right hand on me and said,
"Do not be afraid.
I am the First and the Last."

REVELATION 1:17

WHAT WILL be so amazing about Jesus when we see him in heaven?

Of course, I have no way of answering that question from personal experience. But I can lead you to someone who can. One morning many years ago, a man named John saw Jesus. And what he saw, he recorded, and what he recorded has tantalized seekers of Christ for two thousand years.

To envision John, we should imagine an old man with stooped shoulders and shuffling walk. The years have long passed since he was a young disciple with Jesus in Galilee. His master has been crucified, and most of his friends are dead. And now the Roman government has exiled him to the island of Patmos. Let's imagine him on the beach. He has come here to worship. The wind stirs the cattails, and the waves slap the sand, and John sees nothing but water— an ocean that separates him from his home. But no amount of water could separate him from Christ.

ON THE LORD'S DAY I WAS IN THE SPIRIT, AND I HEARD A LOUD VOICE BEHIND ME THAT SOUNDED LIKE A TRUM-PET. THE VOICE SAID, "WRITE WHAT YOU SEE IN A BOOK AND SEND IT TO THE SEVEN CHURCHES: TO EPHESUS, SMYRNA, PERGAMUM, THYATIRA, SARDIS, PHILADELPHIA, AND LAODICEA." (REV. 1:10–11)

John is about to see Jesus. Of course, this isn't his first time to see his Savior.

You and I only read about

the hands that fed the thousands. Not John. He saw them—knuckled fingers, calloused palms. You and I only read about the feet that found a path through the waves. Not John. John saw them—sandaled, ten-toed, and dirty. You and I only read about his eyes—his flashing eyes, his fiery eyes, his weeping eyes. Not so with John. John saw them. Gazing on the crowds, dancing with laughter, searching for souls. John had seen Jesus.

For three years he'd followed Christ. But this encounter was far different from any in Galilee. The image was so vivid, the impression so powerful, John was knocked out cold: "When I saw him, I fell in a dead faint at his feet" (Rev. 1:17 TJB).

He described the event like this:

I TURNED TO SEE WHO WAS TALKING TO ME. WHEN I TURNED, I SAW SEVEN GOLDEN LAMPSTANDS AND SOMEONE AMONG THE LAMPSTANDS WHO WAS "LIKE A SON OF MAN." HE WAS DRESSED IN A LONG ROBE AND HAD A GOLD BAND AROUND HIS CHEST. HIS HEAD AND HAIR WERE WHITE LIKE WOOL, AS WHITE AS SNOW, AND HIS EYES WERE LIKE FLAMES OF FIRE. HIS FEET WERE LIKE BRONZE THAT GLOWS HOT IN A FURNACE, AND HIS VOICE WAS LIKE THE NOISE OF FLOODING WATER. HE HELD SEVEN STARS IN HIS RIGHT HAND, AND A SHARP DOUBLE-EDGED SWORD CAME OUT OF HIS MOUTH. HE LOOKED LIKE THE SUN SHINING AT ITS BRIGHTEST TIME. WHEN I SAW HIM, I FELL DOWN AT HIS FEET LIKE A DEAD MAN. HE PUT HIS RIGHT HAND ON ME AND SAID, "DO NOT BE AFRAID." (REV. 1:12–17)

If you are puzzled by what you just read, you aren't alone. The world of Revelation cannot be contained or explained; it can only be pondered. And John gave us a vision to ponder, a vision of Christ that comes at us from all angles. A sword and bronze feet and white hair and sunlight. What are we to make of such an image?

First of all, keep in mind that what John wrote is not what he saw. What he wrote is *like* what he saw. But what he saw was so otherworldly that he had no words to describe it.

Consequently, he stumbled into the storage closet of metaphors and returned with an armload of word pictures. Did you notice how often John used the word *like*? He described hair like wool, eyes like fire, feet like bronze, a voice like the noise of flooding water, and then he said Jesus looked like the sun shining at its brightest time. The implication is clear. The human tongue is inadequate to describe Christ. So in a breathless effort to tell us what he saw, John gave us symbols. Symbols originally intended for and understood by members of seven churches in Asia.

For us to comprehend the passage, we must understand the symbols as the original readers understood them.

By the way, John's strategy is not strange. We employ the same. If you open your newspaper to an editorial page and see a donkey talking to an elephant, you know the meaning. You know the symbolism behind the images. And in order for us to understand John's vision, we must do the same. And as we do, as we begin to interpret the pictures, we gain glimpses of what we will see when we see Christ. And it just might knock us out as well!

What John saw was so otherworldly that he had no words to describe it.

THE PERFECT
Priest

*Here is the point of what we are saying:
We have a high priest
who sits on the right side
of God's throne in heaven.*

HEBREWS 8:1

WHEN JOHN saw Jesus in heaven and tried to describe it in Revelation 1, what did he see? When we get to heaven and see Christ, what will we see?

He saw, and we will see, the perfect priest: "He was dressed in a long robe and had a gold band around his chest" (v. 13). The first readers of this message knew the significance of the robe and band. Jesus was wearing the clothing of a priest. A priest presents people to God and God to people.

You have known other priests. There have been others in your life, whether clergy or not, who sought to bring you to God. But they, too, needed a priest. Some needed a priest more than you did. They, like you, were sinful. Not so with Jesus: "Jesus is the kind of high priest we need. He is holy, sinless, pure, not influenced by sinners, and he is raised above the heavens" (Heb. 7:26).

Jesus is the perfect priest.

If a person had never sinned, how would he appear? We'll know when we see Jesus.

He is also pure and purifying: "His head and hair were white like wool, as white as snow, and his eyes were like flames of fire" (Rev. 1:14).

What would a person look like if he had never sinned? If no worry wrinkled his brow and no anger shadowed his eyes? If no bitterness snarled his lips and no selfishness bowed his smile? If a person had never sinned, how would he appear? We'll know when we see Jesus. What John saw on Patmos was absolutely spotless. He was reminded of the virgin wool of sheep and the untouched snow of winter.

And John was also reminded of fire. Others saw the burning bush, the burning altar, the fiery furnace, or the fiery chariots, but John saw the fiery eyes. And in those eyes he saw a purging blaze that will burn the bacteria of sin and purify the soul.

A priest; white-haired, snow-pure, and white-hot. (Already we see this is no pale Galilean.) The image continues, but ponder Jesus as your high priest.

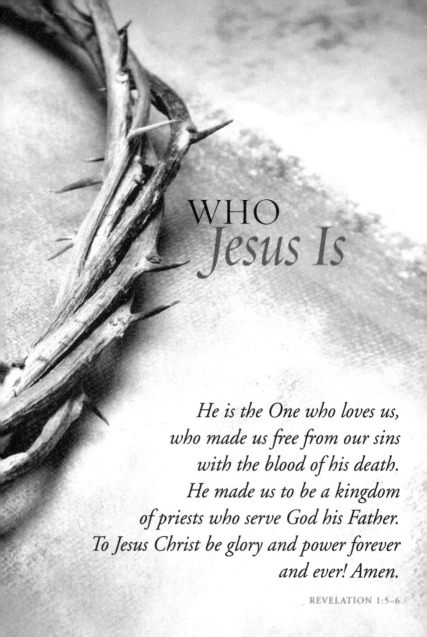

WHO
Jesus Is

He is the One who loves us,
who made us free from our sins
with the blood of his death.
He made us to be a kingdom
of priests who serve God his Father.
To Jesus Christ be glory and power forever
and ever! Amen.

REVELATION 1:5–6

WHEN JOHN saw Jesus in heaven, he saw the perfect priest, but he saw much more. Beholding Jesus, he saw, and we shall see, absolute strength. "His feet were like bronze that glows hot in a furnace" (Rev. 1:15).

John's audience knew the value of this metal. Eugene Peterson helps those of us who don't by explaining:

BRONZE IS A COMBINATION OF IRON AND COPPER. IRON IS STRONG, BUT IT RUSTS. COPPER WON'T RUST, BUT IT'S PLIABLE. COMBINE THE TWO IN BRONZE, AND THE BEST QUALITY OF EACH IS PRESERVED, THE STRENGTH OF THE IRON AND THE ENDURANCE OF THE COPPER. THE RULE OF CHRIST IS SET ON THIS BASE: THE FOUN= DATION OF HIS POWER IS TESTED BY FIRE.[1]

Every power you have ever seen has decayed. The muscle men in the magazines, the automobiles on the racetrack, the armies in the history books. They had their strength, and they had their day, but their day passed. But the strength of Jesus will never be surpassed. Never. When you see him, you will, for the first time, see true strength.

Greed has a growling stomach.

Up until this point, John described what he saw. Now he tells what he heard. He shares the sound of Christ's voice. Not the words, but the sound, the tone, the timbre. The sound of a voice can be more important than the words of a voice. I can say, "I love you," but if I do so with a coerced grumble, you will not feel loved. Ever wonder how you would feel if Jesus spoke to you? John felt like he was near a waterfall: "His voice was like the noise of flooding water" (v. 15).

The sound of a river rushing

through a forest is not a timid one. It is the backdrop of all other sounds. Even when nature sleeps, the river speaks. The same is true of Christ. In heaven his voice is always heard—a steady, soothing, commanding presence.

In his hands were the seven stars. "He held seven stars in his right hand" (v. 16). We later read that "the seven stars are the angels of the seven churches" (v. 20). With apologies to southpaws, the right hand in Scripture is the picture of readiness. Joseph was blessed by Jacob's right hand (Gen. 48:18), the Red Sea was divided when God stretched out his right hand (Ex. 15:12), the right hand of God sustains us (Ps. 18:35), and Jesus is at the right hand of God interceding (Rom. 8:34). The right hand is a picture of action. And what did John see in the right hand of Christ? The angels of the churches. Like a soldier readies his sword or a carpenter grips his hammer, Jesus secures the angels, ready to send them to protect his people.

How welcome is this reassurance! How good to know that the pure, fiery, bronze-footed Son of Man has one priority: the protection of his churches. He holds them in the palm of his right hand. And he directs them with the sword of his word: "And a sharp double-edged sword came out of his mouth" (Rev. 1:16).

The sound of his voice soothes the soul, but the truth of his voice pierces the soul:

GOD'S WORD IS ALIVE AND WORKING AND IS SHARPER THAN A DOUBLE-EDGED SWORD. IT CUTS ALL THE WAY INTO US, WHERE THE SOUL AND SPIRIT ARE JOINED, TO THE CENTER OF OUR JOINTS AND BONES. AND IT JUDGES THE THOUGHTS AND FEELINGS IN OUR HEARTS. NOTHING IN ALL THE WORLD CAN BE HIDDEN FROM GOD. (HEB. 4:12–13)

No more charades.
No more games.
No more half-truths.

Heaven is an honest land. It is a land where the shadows are banished by the face of Christ: "His face was like the sun shining in all its brilliance" (Rev. 1:16 NIV).

What are we to do with such a picture? How are we to assimilate these images? Are we to combine them on a canvas and consider it a portrait of Jesus? I don't think so. I don't think the goal of this vision is to tell us what Jesus looks like but who Jesus is:

> the Perfect Priest;
> the Only Pure One;
> the Source of Strength;
> the Sound of Love;
> the Everlasting Light.

What will happen
WHEN YOU

SEE JESUS?

You will see unblemished purity and unbending strength. You will feel his unending presence and know his unbridled protection. And all that he is, you will be, for you will be like Jesus. Wasn't that the promise of John? "We know that when Christ comes again, we will be like him, because we will see him as he really is" (1 John 3:2).

Since you'll be as pure as snow, you will never sin again.

Since you'll be as strong as bronze, you will never stumble again.

Since you'll dwell near the river, you will never feel lonely again.

Since the work of the priest will have been finished, you will never doubt again.

In heaven, you will dwell in the light of God. And you will see him as he really is.

WHILE
We Wait

There are many rooms in my Father's house;
I would not tell you this if it were not true.
I am going there to prepare a place for you.
After I go and prepare a place for you,
I will come back and take you to be with me
so that you may be where I am.

JOHN 14:2–3

ARE WE not the bride of Christ? Have we not been set apart "as a pure bride to one husband" (2 Cor. 11:2 NLT)? Did God not say to us, "I will make you my promised bride forever" (Hos. 2:19)?

We are engaged to our Maker! We, the peasants, have heard the promise of the Prince. He entered our village, took our hands, and stole our hearts. Why, even the angels inclined their ears to hear us say, "Yes."

He is building a house for you. And with every swing of the hammer and cut of the saw, he's dreaming of the day he carries you over the threshold.

You have been chosen by Christ. You are released from your old life in your old house, and he has claimed you as his beloved. "Then where is he?" you might ask. "Why hasn't he come?"

There is only one answer. His bride is not ready. She is still being prepared.

Engaged people are obsessed with preparation. The right dress. The right weight. The right hair and the right tux. They want everything to be right. Why? So their fiancées will marry them? No. Just the opposite. They want to look their best because their fiancées are marrying them.

The same is true for us.

You are spoken for. You are engaged, set apart, called out, a holy bride.

We want to look our best for Christ. We want our hearts to be pure and our thoughts to be clean. We want our faces to shine with grace and our eyes to sparkle with love. We want to be prepared.

Why? In hopes that he will love us? No. Just the opposite. Because he already does.

You are spoken for. You are engaged, set apart, called out, a holy bride. You have been chosen for his castle. Don't settle for one-night stands in the arms of strangers.

Be obsessed with your wedding date. Guard against forgetfulness. Write yourself notes. Memorize verses. Do whatever you need to do to remember. "Aim at what is in heaven. . . . Think only about the things in heaven" (Col. 3:1–2). You are engaged to royalty, and your Prince is coming to take you home!

CHAPTER 3: FIX YOUR WARDROBE

1. Augustus M. Toplady, "Rock of Ages."
2. Edward Mote, "The Solid Rock."

CHAPTER 5: THE BRAND-NEW YOU

1. Unless you are alive when Christ returns, and then you will also get a new body (1 Cor. 15:51).

CHAPTER 7: GROANING IN THE TENT

1. Hans-Joachim Kraus, *Charisma der Theologie*, as quoted in John Piper, *Future Grace* (Sisters, OR: Multnomah Books, 1995), 370.
2. Joni Eareckson Tada, *Heaven: Your Real Home* (Grand Rapids: Zondervan, 1995), 39.

CHAPTER 8: LIKE JESUS

1. Luke 24:13–35; John 20:10–18; 21:12–14.
2. John 20:14; 21:1–4; Luke 24:16; John 20:26.

CHAPTER 16: SEEING JESUS

1. Peter Kreeft, *Heaven: The Heart's Deepest Longing* (San Francisco: Ignatius Press, 1980), 49.

CHAPTER 19: WHO JESUS IS

1. Eugene Peterson, *Reversed Thunder* (San Francisco: HarperSanFrancisco, 1988), 36–37.

NO ONE

has ever imagined

WHAT GOD HAS PREPARED

for those who love him.